THEMES for early years PHOTOCOPIABLES

THE WORLD AROUND US

EDITOR

Susan Howard

ASSISTANT EDITOR

Lesley Sudlow

ILLUSTRATOR

Jo Moore

COVER

Lynne Joesbury

SERIES DESIGNER

Sarah Rock

DESIGNER

Rachael Hammond

AUTHOR

Sally Gray

Published by Scholastic Ltd,
Villiers House, Clarendon Avenue,
Leamington Spa, Warwickshire CV32 5PR

© 2000 Scholastic Ltd Text © 2000 Sally Gray
1 2 3 4 5 6 7 8 9   0 1 2 3 4 5 6 7 8 9

The publishers gratefully acknowledge the British Deaf Association for the colour signs
reproduced in this book

British Library Cataloguing-in-Publication Data
A catalogue record for this book is available from the British Library.

ISBN 0-439-01742-4

CONTENTS

INTRODUCTION
PAGE 5

COLOURS

TEACHERS' NOTES
PAGE 7

Streetwise **10**
Little red book **11**
Animal colours **12**
Into the ark **13**
Party plates **14**
Favourite colours **15**
Seaside colours **16**
Tricolour flags **17**
Colour signs **18**
What colour am I? **19**
Down in the jungle **20**
Colour spinner **21**
Colour dice **22**
Mosaics **23**
The paint shop **24**

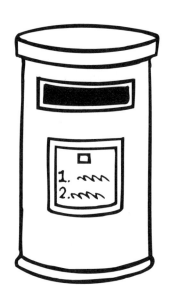

SHAPES

TEACHERS' NOTES
PAGE 25

Curvy or straight? **28**
Shape books **29**
Fat and thin **30**
Shapes all around **31**
Shape dominoes **32**
Shapes and sizes **33**
Count the sides **34**
Shape castles **35**
Roll or slide? **36**
Leaf shapes **37**
Build the model **38**
Thread a shape **39**
Shape flowers **40**
Spin a shape **41**
Butterfly patterns **42**

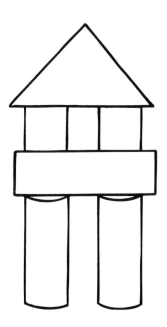

PEOPLE WHO HELP US

TEACHERS' NOTES
PAGE 43

People poster **46**
Emergency **47**
Make it better **48**
Friends **49**
People puzzles **50**
Washing day **51**
Sort the post **52**
Certificate **53**
I can help **54**
No more rubbish **55**
Animals that help us **56**
A helping hand **57**
People puppets **58**
Dressing-up **59**
At the clinic **60**

JOURNEYS

TEACHERS' NOTES
PAGE 61

Lift-the-flap **64**
Follow the trail **65**
At the park **66**
Pack the bag **67**
Count the passengers **68**
Air, land or sea **69**
Journey to the moon **70**
A world of food **71**
Local journey **72**
On the map **73**
Picture postcards **74**
Transport **75**
Flying high **76**
Storyboard **77**
Billy goat puppets **78**

WEATHER

TEACHERS' NOTES
PAGE 79

Incy Wincy Spider **82**
Wet and dry **83**
Weather dice **84**
Nursery rhyme spinner **85**
Scarf patterns **86**
Umbrellas **87**
Weather wear **88**
Snowmen **89**
Dressing bear **90**
Weather chart **91**
Weather symbols **92**
Windmill **93**
Sounds like rain **94**
Sun-hat **95**
Seaside kiosk **96**

INTRODUCTION

Using themes

The *Themes for Early Years Photocopiable* series builds on and supplements the existing *Themes for Early Years* series, providing practitioners with a rich source of material for their topic planning and delivery.

The World Around Us is designed to link closely to five of the original *Themes* titles, building on the ideas and providing additional material to broaden the scope of each of the topics. The books may be used together, but *The World Around Us* is also a useful resource in its own right.

The theme of *The World Around Us* is a broad and varied topic that covers many of the settings, experiences and emotions familiar to early years children. The children will be given opportunities to explore and develop their understanding in this essential topic as they take part in lively games, discussions, stories, rhymes and activities.

How to use this book

The World Around Us combines the original *Themes* titles: *Colours*; *Shapes*; *People Who Help Us*; *Journeys* and *Weather* in one book. Each of these sub-themes has its own eighteen-page chapter, providing fifteen new photocopiable activity sheets and three pages of accompanying teachers' notes. The activity ideas are simple, effective and child-friendly, giving clear, concise instructions and allowing the children enough space to explore their ideas.

The activities in this book are clearly linked with QCA's Early Learning Goals. They comprehensively cover the six Areas of Learning and every learning objective closely matches the QCA document, enabling practitioners to monitor their coverage of the curriculum. In addition, the activities provide clear and valuable opportunities to assess the children. The teachers' notes offer a complete lesson plan for each photocopiable sheet, explaining how to use the sheet and how to introduce, conclude and differentiate the activity.

Using the photocopiable sheets

To maximize the potential of the photocopiable sheets, it is important to use them in conjunction with the accompanying teachers' notes. The notes not only explain the main use for the sheet, but also provide suggestions for introducing, differentiating and reinforcing the concept. The children will benefit more from the work if the sheet is presented with some adult input and often they are intended for groups or pairs as well as individuals.

The photocopiable sheets are designed to be used in a number of ways – suggestions are sometimes made to enlarge the sheet or to copy it onto card or coloured paper. You may also choose to laminate some of the sheets, particularly those that will be used as games or for visual stimuli to promote discussion.

Many of the photocopiable sheets may be used several times, as they have been written as open-ended tasks and can be reapplied with a new theme or subject matter. For example, some of the sheets are designed to be used in role-play settings and provide templates for the children to use on a regular basis. Several of the mathematics activities can be used with a different number or mathematical operation focus or as games.

Assessment

Date and keep copies of some of the photocopiable sheets once the children have used them. They are an important assessment tool and can be kept as records that demonstrate your coverage of the curriculum. You may also like to plan an assessment activity in advance, using one of the sheets as a way of recording the children's progress. For example, if you are planning to assess the children's ability to sort objects to more than one criteria, use the 'Sort the post' activity (page 52) to note how many different criteria they can employ and how well they can explain their groupings. Date the work and add your own notes on the reverse.

A variety of resources

The activities in this book have been designed to be used with a broad range of materials and resources readily found in early years settings. In completing these activities, the children will be using collage materials, pens and pencils, scissors, malleable and construction materials and simple tools, such as scissors and mark-making implements.

The photocopiable sheets will provide the children with many opportunities to develop a broad range of essential early learning skills from turn-taking in counting games, to retelling stories and rhymes and making books.

Links with home

The theme of *The World Around Us* has many natural links with the children's homes and families. Through these activities, the children will have opportunities to learn and talk about their local area, people who help them, past experiences in their own lives, and the weather. The photocopiable sheets make it easy to share this work and include the children's own families in their learning and discovery. Let the children take some of their finished work home with them and occasionally send home some of the activities for the children to share with their parents or siblings. Make sure that you have talked to the parents about the learning potential of the activities, but explain that the activities, although educational, should always be made fun, with an emphasis on play.

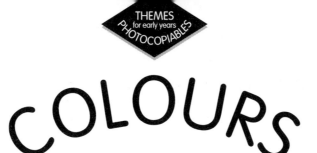

COLOURS

PAGE 10

STREETWISE

Learning objective
To talk about experiences and develop descriptive vocabulary. (Language and Literacy)
Group size
Whole group; individuals.

During circle time, ask the children to close their eyes and imagine their local town. Now say the name of a colour and ask them to think of something in their town that is the same colour, such as a 'green tree' and so on. Show the children a copy of the photocopiable sheet enlarged to A3 size. Ask them to describe the things that they can see. Does the picture remind them of a place they know? What colours might the objects in the picture be in real life? Provide each child with a copy of the photocopiable sheet and encourage them to colour it in appropriate colours.

PAGE 11

LITTLE RED BOOK

Learning objective
To use pictures and letters to communicate meaning. (Language and Literacy)
Group size
Small groups.

Share a book about colours with the children, such as *My First Look at Colours* (Dorling Kindersley). Give each child a copy of the photocopiable sheet and explain that they are going to make a little book about the colour red. Help them to cut along the lines as indicated. Put the first strip on top of the second and fold inwards along the centre line to produce a little book with eight pages. On the cover, write 'My little red book by...'. Encourage the children to turn the pages of their book and to colour the tomato and post-box red. Now ask them to think of five more red things to draw and colour on the blank pages, depending on their ability. Encourage older children to have a go at writing the words underneath.

PAGE 12

ANIMAL COLOURS

Learning objective
To develop descriptive vocabulary and to use pictures to communicate meaning. (Language and Literacy)
Group size
Small groups.

Gather the children together to share some information books about animals. Talk about the animals and encourage the children to describe them. Give each child a copy of the photocopiable sheet and identify the animals together. What colours are the animals in real life? Suggest that older children use the information books to find out and then colour the pictures on the sheet to match. Enlarge the sheet for younger children and give them a choice of one or two animals. Find the animals in a book to show them.

PAGE 13

INTO THE ARK

Learning objective
To develop sequencing and story-telling skills. (Language and Literacy)
Group size
Up to six children.

Tell the children the story of 'Noah's Ark' (found in all good children's bibles). Talk about rainbows with the children. Have any of them ever seen one? Who knows what colours are in a rainbow? Now provide each child with a copy of the photocopiable sheet. Cut out the pictures and decide together on the correct order of the pictures. Encourage the children to retell the story as they colour the pictures and stick them in order in small home-made books or on a sheet of paper. Scribe the words for them and encourage older children to have a go at the writing themselves.

PAGE 14

PARTY PLATES

Learning objective
To develop matching and counting skills. (Mathematical Development)
Group size
Small groups.

Stock the home corner with plenty of brightly-coloured plastic plates and pretend fruit and vegetables. Encourage the children, in their play, to sort the fruit and vegetables by colour. Are any of them the same colour as the plates? Can they match them up? Provide each

child with a copy of the photocopiable sheet and explain that you would like them to colour one plate green and the other yellow. Ask them to identify the food. What colours are they? Ask them to cut out the food and to match each piece to the coloured plates. Ask older children to draw at least one more item of food for each plate.

FAVOURITE COLOURS

PAGE 15

Learning objective
To develop comparing, ordering and counting skills. (Mathematical Development)
Group size
Up to five children.

As a group, decide on up to five colours to include in a favourite colours graph. Enlarge the photocopiable sheet to A3 size and write the colour words in the boxes on the horizontal axis. Colour them in to match. Now demonstrate how to fill in the graph by asking each child in the group to choose their favourite colour from the selection. As each child tells you their choice, colour in a square above the colour name. Count the results together and use the opportunity to develop comparative language (such as 'more than' and 'most'). Use the sheet for recording other colour surveys, such as eye or hair colour.

SEASIDE COLOURS

PAGE 16

Learning objective
To develop recognition of numbers to six. (Mathematical Development)
Group size
Individuals.

Send a copy of the photocopiable sheet home at the beginning of the summer holidays. Explain to parents that by doing this fun activity, the children will be developing their number recognition and problem-solving skills. Suggest that they begin by reading the colour words to their child and asking them to lightly colour the number boxes with the appropriate colour, then help their child to use the key to colour in the picture.

TRICOLOUR FLAGS

PAGE 17

If possible look at some pictures of flags with the children – many children's atlases provide a good selection. Talk about the colours and patterns of the flags together. Provide each child with a copy of the photocopiable sheet. Ask them to choose three colours and explain that they may use only these three colours (one for each stripe) to colour the flags and that they may use each colour only once per flag. Ask them to try to make each flag different. Demonstrate by colouring one of the flags, for example red, yellow and blue. The next one might be red, blue and yellow and so on. By doing this activity, the children will be developing skills of ordering, logic and pattern.

Learning objective
To use developing mathematical understanding to solve simple practical problems. (Mathematical Development)
Group size
Small groups.

COLOUR SIGNS

PAGE 18

Talk to the children about their senses and ask them to try to imagine what it would be like if they couldn't hear. (NB Be sensitive to individual children's circumstances.) Explain that there is a special language called sign language that people can use so that deaf people can understand without having to hear any words. Explain that you are going to learn some of these special signs for colours. Enlarge a copy of the photocopiable sheet to show to the children and, over time, teach them the colour signs. Once the children are confident with the signs, use them to sign along as they sing the song 'I can sing a rainbow'. Arrange to sing for a local deaf club or at a special school.

Learning objective
To learn about others' disabilities and to show sensitivity to the needs of others. (Personal, Social and Emotional Development)
Group size
Whole group.

PAGE 19
WHAT COLOUR AM I?

Learning objective
To work as part of a group, taking turns and sharing fairly. (Personal, Social and Emotional Development)
Group size
Up to four children.

Bring in a selection of fruit and vegetables to show to the children. Together, sort them in different ways – by colour, shape and food type. Give each child a copy of the photocopiable sheet, identify the pictures and say what colour each one is. Cover a dice with coloured stickers (orange, yellow, green, red, purple and brown). Let the children take it in turns to throw the dice and colour the fruit or vegetable that matches the colour on the dice. Emphasize the process of taking turns and encourage the children to pass each other the dice. Make two copies of the photocopiable sheet and let older children cut out the picture cards and play a game of pairs or pelmanism with a partner.

PAGE 20
DOWN IN THE JUNGLE

Learning objective
To learn about features of living things. (Knowledge and Understanding of the World)
Group size
Whole group; individuals.

Introduce the activity by singing the song 'Down in the jungle where nobody goes' in *This Little Puffin*, compiled by Elizabeth Matterson (Puffin). Enlarge a copy of the photocopiable sheet to A3 size. Show the children the picture and talk about jungle animals together. What colours are the animals in real life? Which ones are bright colours? Which ones are the same colours as the plants so that they can hide (camouflage)? Give each child a copy of the photocopiable sheet and help them to choose the correct colours to colour the animals. Ask older children to use information books to help them.

PAGE 21
COLOUR SPINNER

Learning objective
To use cutting and building skills for a variety of purposes. (Knowledge and Understanding of the World)
Group size
Small groups.

Help each child to make their own colour spinner. Copy the photocopiable sheet onto card and help the children to colour each section in its appropriate colour. Help them to pierce the spinner with a pencil to use as the spinning axis. Encourage the children to play some games with the spinners. Ask each child in turn to spin their spinner. Ask them to say the colour it lands on

and then set them a colour challenge, such as building a tower from red bricks or finding three green objects and so on.

PAGE 22
COLOUR DICE

Learning objectives
To use appropriate tools with safety and increasing control; to develop manipulative skills. (Physical Development)
Group size
Small groups.

Copy the photocopiable sheet onto thin card and give one copy to each child. Ask them to colour the fruit and vegetables in the appropriate colours. Help them to cut out the net shape and stick it together to make a dice. Let them take it in turns to throw the dice, identify the object and say its colour name. Now ask all the children in the group to model the fruit or vegetable from Plasticine. Repeat the process until all the children have had a turn.

PAGE 23
MOSAICS

Learning objective
To explore colour and form in two dimensions. (Creative Development)
Group size
Individuals.

Look at some mosaics and tiles with the children – either real or in pictures. Talk about the colours, patterns and textures that they can see. Provide each child with a copy of the photocopiable sheet and ask them to look carefully at the mosaic tiles. Can they see the picture? Ask them to colour in or use collage to make the flower stand out from the rest of the tiles.

PAGE 24
THE PAINT SHOP

Learning objective
To explore colour through imaginative play. (Creative Development)
Group size
Up to four children.

Develop your role-play area into a DIY shop. Provide children's tool kits, paintbrushes, paint trays, buckets, old wallpaper rolls and so on. Set up a nearby table with paints, brushes and mixing trays. Suggest that the children can mix the paint colours they wish to buy. Provide copies of the photocopiable sheet for them to record their paint mixing. Suggest that they paint squares of the colours used for mixing such as blue, yellow and white on the paint pots, and on the chart underneath put dabs of the colours that they created. Ask older children to invent and write imaginative names for their colours, such as sandy-beach yellow or jungle-fern green!

Streetwise

◆ Talk about the picture. What colours should things be?

Little red book

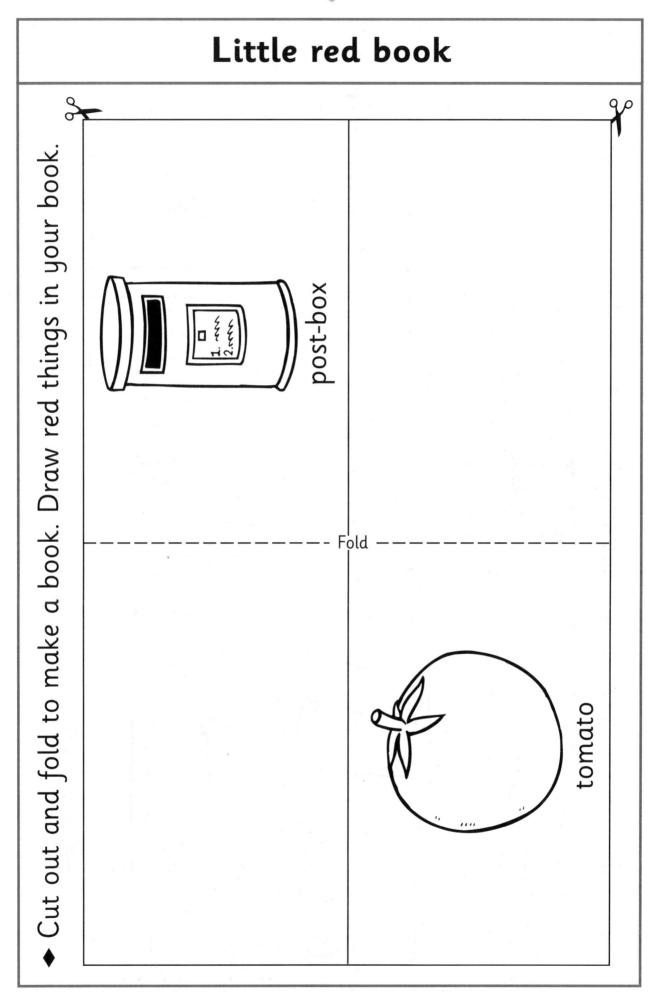

◆ Cut out and fold to make a book. Draw red things in your book.

post-box

Fold

tomato

Animal colours

◆ Find out the colours of these animals and colour them in.

butterfly

dolphin

starfish

ladybird

goldfish

parrot

Into the ark

◆ Cut out the pictures and put them in the correct order. Tell the story.

Party plates

◆ Colour the food and the plates in the correct colour. Match the food to the plates.

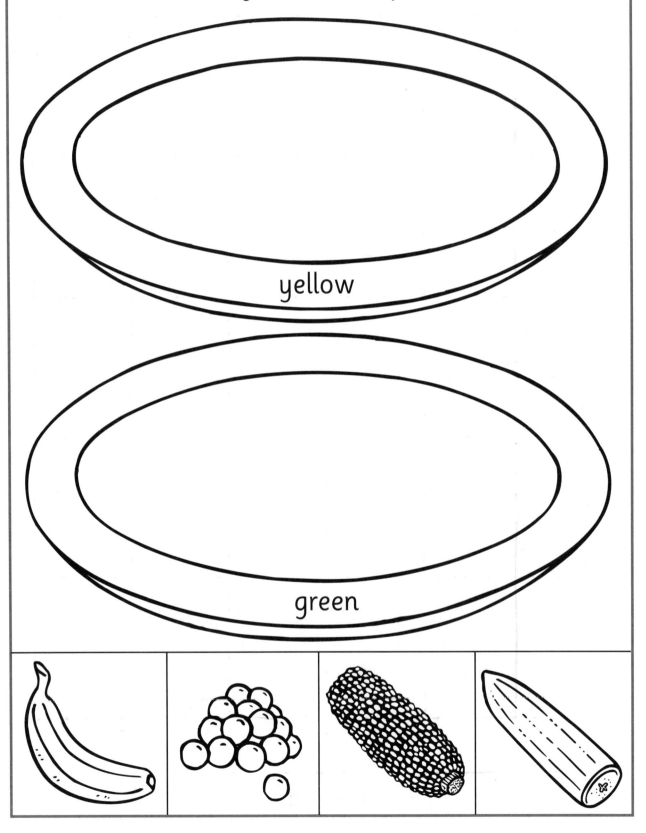

yellow

green

Favourite colours

◆ Use the block graph to record people's favourite colours.

5					
4					
3					
2					
1					

numbers

colours

Seaside colours

◆ Use the key to colour the picture.

1 = blue 2 = green 3 = red 4 = yellow 5 = white 6 = orange

Tricolour flags

◆ Use three colours only to colour the stripes on the flags. Make each flag different.

Colour signs

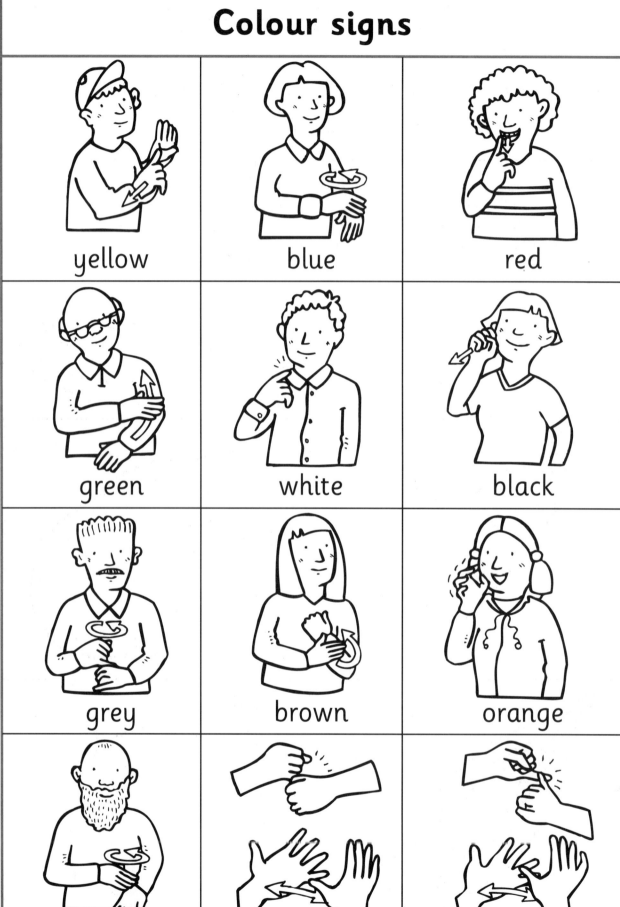

yellow	blue	red
green	white	black
grey	brown	orange
purple	gold	silver

What colour am I?

◆ Throw the dice and match the picture.
Colour the fruit or vegetable.

Down in the jungle

Talk about the picture. Find out what colours the plants and animals should be.

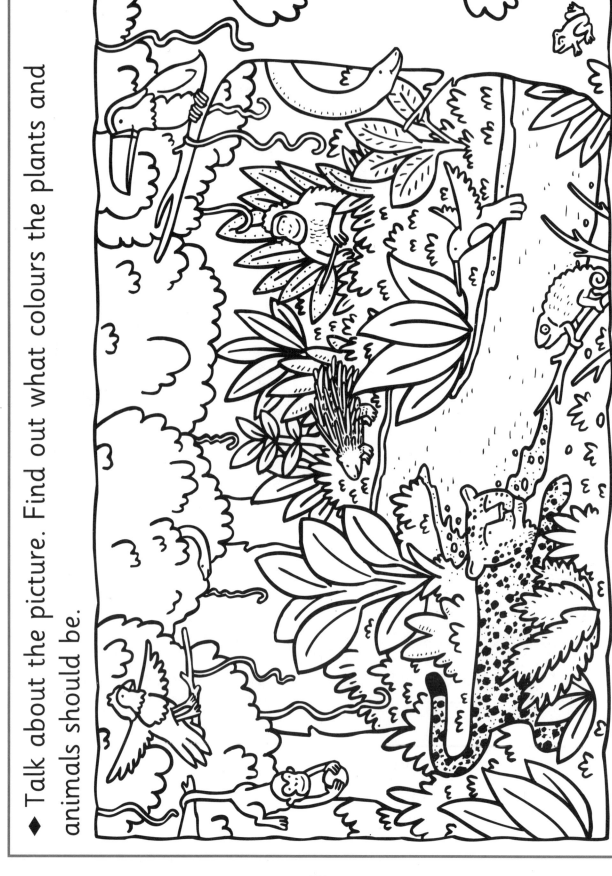

Colour spinner

◆ Make the spinner. Use it to play some colour games.

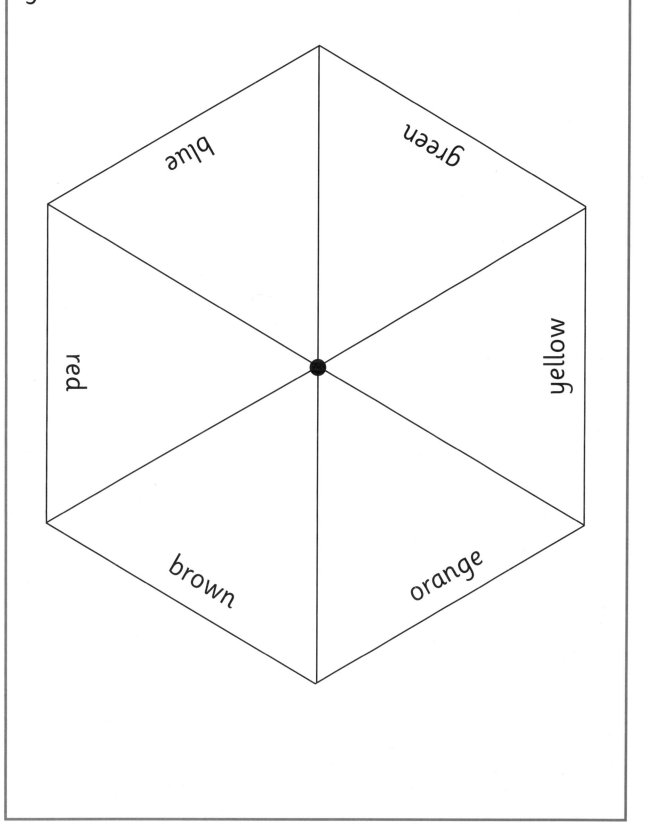

Colour dice

◆ Colour and cut out to make a colour dice.

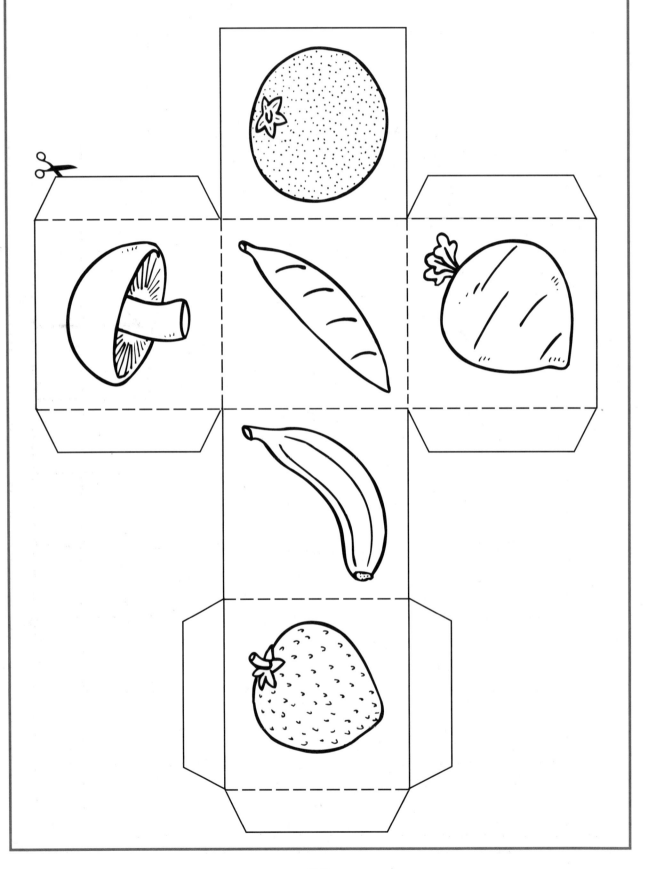

Mosaics

◆ Find the flower. Decorate it carefully.

The paint shop

◆ Record your paint mixing work here.
I used these colours:

paint chart

SHAPES

PAGE 28
CURVY OR STRAIGHT?

Learning objective
To develop descriptive vocabulary. (Language and Literacy)
Group size Small groups.

Show the children a selection of objects such as a ball, ruler, spoon and pencil, and put them inside a feely bag. Put your hand inside the bag and describe one of the objects. Can the children guess what it is? Now let them take turns to put their hand inside the bag and to feel and describe an object. Encourage them to use words such as curvy, straight, flat, bumpy and so on. Give each child a copy of the photocopiable sheet and ask them to identify the objects. Suggest that they colour all the curvy things blue and all the straight things red. You could also use the sheet to play 'Kim's game', where the children have to remember as many of the objects as they can when they can no longer see them.

PAGE 29
SHAPE BOOKS

Learning objective
To use pictures and symbols to communicate meaning. (Language and Literacy)
Group size Small groups.

Share a pop-up or novelty book with the children and draw their attention to the shapes that have been used to make the book. Give each child a copy of the photocopiable sheet and show them how to cut out and fold the pages to make a shape zigzag book. Talk about the shapes together. Let older children use the shapes to inspire an imaginative story and encourage younger children to draw pointed, round and straight objects on the relevant pages. Scribe the words for the children if necessary.

PAGE 30
FAT AND THIN

Share an action rhyme about animals with the children, such as 'An elephant goes like this and that' in *This Little Puffin* compiled by Elizabeth Matterson (Puffin). Encourage the children to think about the size and shape of different animals. If possible, look at some pictures of different animals and talk about their shapes.. Give each child a copy of the photocopiable sheet – the pictures show a fat animal and a small animal. Explain that you would like them to draw a thin animal and a big animal in the spaces. Use the pictures to begin a group animal shapes book.

Learning objective
To develop the vocabulary of size and shape and to use pictures and symbols to communicate meaning. (Language and Literacy)
Group size Small groups.

PAGE 31
SHAPES ALL AROUND

During circle time, explain to the children that you would like them to look around the room and see what shapes they can see. Call out the name of a shape such as square, and invite individual children to find an example from around the room, point to it and describe it. Enlarge a copy of the photocopiable sheet and talk about the scene with the children. Ask them to tell you about any shapes that they can see. Give each child a copy of the photocopiable sheet and ask them to colour in the picture, using different colours for the different shapes. Encourage older children to call the shapes by their correct names.

Learning objective
To develop speaking and listening skills. (Language and Literacy)
Group size Whole group; individuals.

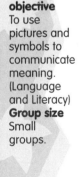

PAGE 32
SHAPE DOMINOES

Learning objective
To develop shape recognition skills. (Mathematical Development)
Group size
Pairs.

Copy the photocopiable sheet onto card and give each child a copy. Ask them to cut out the dominoes to make a set. In pairs, let the children combine their sets, muddle them up and use them to play a version of the dominoes game. Explain the following rules.
• The first player places a domino on the table.
• The next player must match the shape at one end of the domino. If they cannot, they must miss a go.
• The winner is the first person to get rid of all their dominoes.

PAGE 33
SHAPES AND SIZES

Learning objective
To develop shape recognition, matching and ordering skills. (Mathematical Development)
Group size
Small groups; individuals.

Remind the children of the properties and names of triangles and squares and show them some plastic or card shapes. Copy the photocopiable sheet onto card for each child and ask them to cut out the cards. Ask them to complete some of the following tasks.
• Sort the cards into sets using shape or size as the criteria.
• Play a game of shape snap with a friend.
• Put the squares in order of size.
• Make some shape repeating patterns.

PAGE 34
COUNT THE SIDES

Learning objective
To develop counting and shape recognition skills. (Mathematical Development)
Group size
Small groups; individuals.

Provide a selection of sorting shapes for the children to look at. Practise sorting the shapes according to different specified criteria. Test the children's comprehension by making a group of shapes, one of which is different in some way (for example, a set of shapes with four sides and one triangle). Which is the odd one out?

Give each child a copy of the photocopiable sheet and ask them to cut out the shapes carefully. Invite them to count the sides and sort them into two sets based on the number of sides. Cut out the shapes for younger children and count the sides by drawing a coloured line along each side as you count.

PAGE 35
SHAPE CASTLES

Learning objective
To work co-operatively with a partner. (Personal, Social and Emotional Development)
Group size
Pairs.

Give each pair of children an enlarged copy of the photocopiable sheet and talk about the different shapes together. Ask the children to cut out the shapes and to share out three shapes each. Now ask them to work together to make a castle shape, using the picture at the bottom of the photocopiable sheet as reference. Encourage the children to use drawn or gummed shapes to decorate the castle. Challenge older children to use shapes to make an extra wing and outbuildings for the castle.

PAGE 36
ROLL OR SLIDE?

Learning objective
To explore and recognize the features of three-dimensional shapes. (Knowledge and Understanding of the World)
Group size
Small groups.

Provide a selection of three-dimensional shapes for the children to investigate. Encourage them to handle each of the shapes, describing how it feels. Provide each child with a copy of the photocopiable sheet and explain that you are going to find out which shapes slide and which shapes roll. Set up a simple ramp, such as a large book tilted on some bricks. Encourage the children to use the recording sheet to make predictions and to record their results. Ask older children to explain their predictions and help younger children by acting as scribe.

PAGE 37
LEAF SHAPES

Learning objective
To look closely at the similarities and differences of objects in the natural world. (Knowledge and Understanding of the World)
Group size
Whole group; individuals.

Take the children for a walk to an area with a variety of trees. Encourage them to observe the different shapes that they can see in the trees – branches, trunks, bark patterns and leaves. Collect some different-shaped fallen leaves if possible. Back inside, explain to the children that different types of tree have different-shaped leaves. Ask the children to describe the leaves you have brought back. Give each child a copy of the photocopiable sheet and ask them to cut out, describe and sort the leaves into sets such as rounded, pointy and so on. Help older children to identify them in nature guides, using shape as the classifying criteria.

PAGE 38
BUILD THE MODEL

Learning objective
To explore and select construction materials and develop building skills. (Knowledge and Understanding of the World)
Group size
Small groups.

Let the children play freely with a set of shape bricks. Encourage them to sort the bricks into shape sets. Ask them to name the different shapes and describe their properties. Enlarge a copy of the photocopiable sheet to show to the children and ask them to tell you about the pictures. What shapes have been used? What are the models of? Challenge the children to use the shape bricks to copy the pictures. Let younger children choose just one or two to copy and challenge older children to add extra models of their own on the reverse of the sheet.

PAGE 39
THREAD A SHAPE

Learning objective
To handle tools and objects with increasing control. (Physical Development)
Group size
Individuals.

Copy the photocopiable sheet onto card for each child. Ask the children to cut out the shape and help them to make the holes where indicated, using a hole-punch or bradawl (adults only). Provide the children with a blunt tapestry needle, threaded with thick thread or ribbon and ask them to thread through the holes, following the shape. To extend the activity, number the holes around the shape in a haphazard fashion and ask the children to join the holes in number order.

PAGE 40
SHAPE FLOWERS

Learning objective
To explore colour, shape and form. (Creative Development)
Group size
Whole group; individuals.

Teach the children the rhyme 'Mary, Mary, Quite Contrary' (Traditional). Ask the children to draw a picture of Mary's garden. Can they describe the shapes that they used in their flowers? What colours and patterns did they use? Copy the photocopiable sheet onto card for each child. Ask them to describe the flower shapes. Let them colour in the shapes and cut them out. Help the children to attach the flowers to dowelling rods wrapped in green tissue paper. Stick them into lumps of Plasticine and display them in flower pots or decorated yoghurt pots. Use the flowers to make repeating patterns and for counting and matching activities.

PAGE 41
SPIN A SHAPE

Copy the photocopiable sheet onto card and cut out the spinner. Cut out the arrow shape and fix it loosely to the centre of the spinner with a split pin. Use the shape spinner for a variety of activities.
• Take it in turns to spin a shape. Provide a set of shape tiles and ask the children to collect a matching tile. When they have collected a few shapes, encourage the children to make a shape picture from them.
• Spin a shape, describe it and copy it onto paper. Now ask the children to try to make that shape with their bodies, for example by curling into a ball for a circle, stretching up high for a rectangle and so on.

Learning objective
To explore shape and form in two and three dimensions. (Creative Development)
Group size
Small groups; individuals.

PAGE 42
BUTTERFLY PATTERNS

Look at some pictures of butterflies together. Point out to the children how a butterfly has the same pattern on both of its wings. Ask the children to describe the shapes and patterns on the different butterflies. Provide each child with a copy of the photocopiable sheet and explain that you would like them to draw some patterns onto the butterfly's wings. Encourage them to draw the same pattern on each of the wings. Challenge older children to include a certain number of specified shapes and help younger children to match the wings by drawing a shape at a time onto each wing.

Learning objective
To explore colour, shape and form. (Creative Development)
Group size
Individuals.

Curvy or straight?

◆ Describe the objects. Colour the curvy things blue and the straight things red.

Shape books

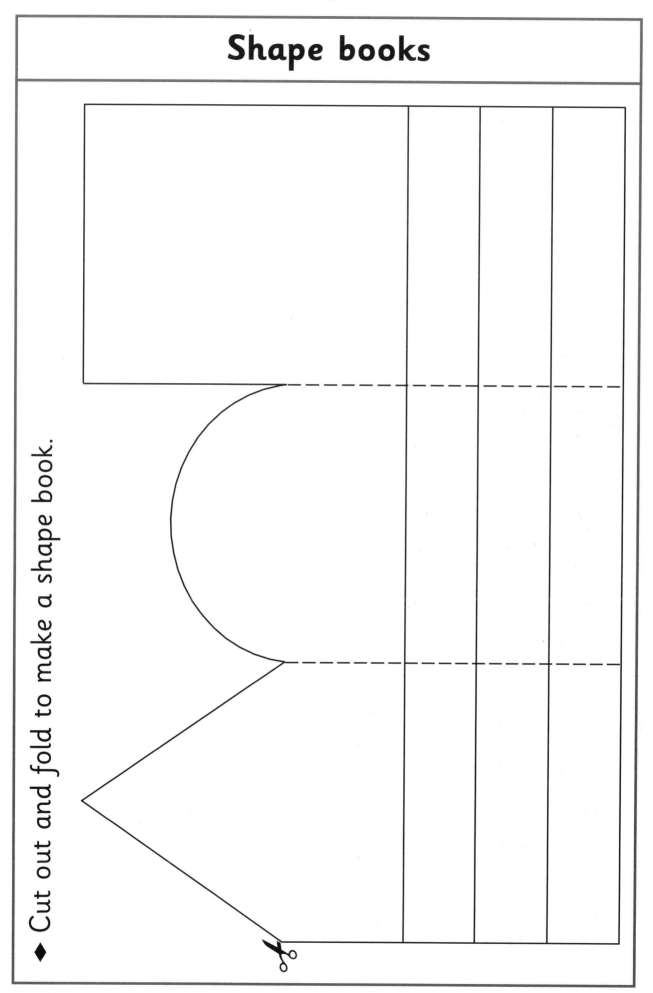

Cut out and fold to make a shape book.

Fat and thin

◆ Draw a thin animal and a big animal.

fat

thin

big

small

Shapes all around

♦ Talk about the shapes that you can see.

Shape dominoes

◆ Cut out and use to play matching games.

Shapes and sizes

◆ Cut out, sort, match and use the cards for games.

Count the sides

◆ Cut out the shapes, count the sides and sort them into sets.

Shape castles

◆ Work with a partner. Cut out the shapes and make a castle.

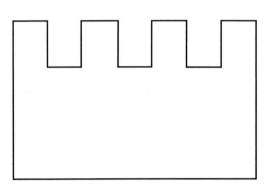

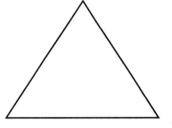

Roll or slide?

◆ Try out some shapes on a ramp. Guess if they will roll or slide.

Shape	I think it will roll	I think it will slide	What I found out
cylinder			
pyramid			
cube			
sphere			
cuboid			

Leaf shapes

◆ Look at the leaves and describe them.

Build the model

◆ Describe the pictures. What shapes can you see? Make the models.

Thread a shape

◆ Cut out the shape and thread it carefully.

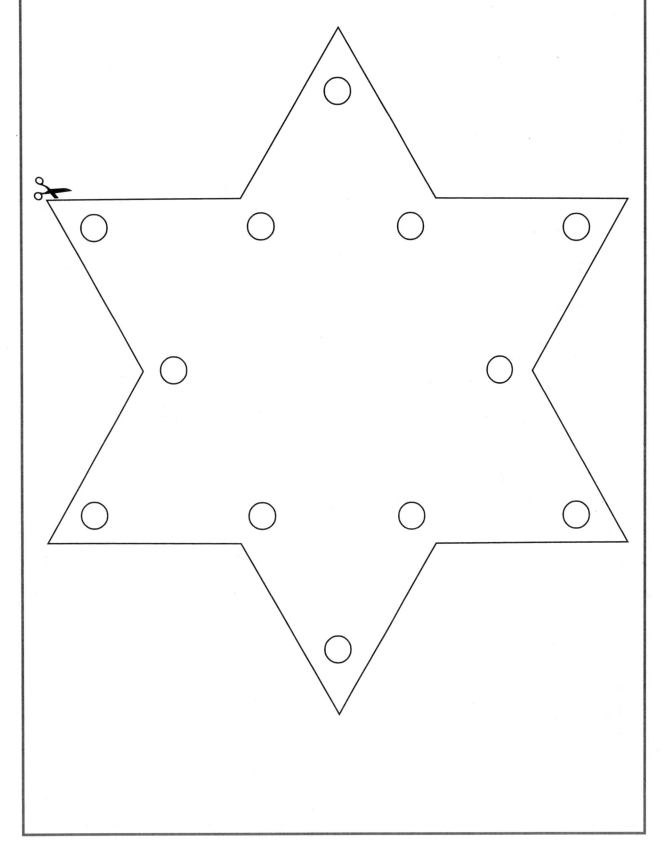

Shape flowers

◆ Colour in the shapes and cut out.

Spin a shape

◆ Cut out and make into a spinner.

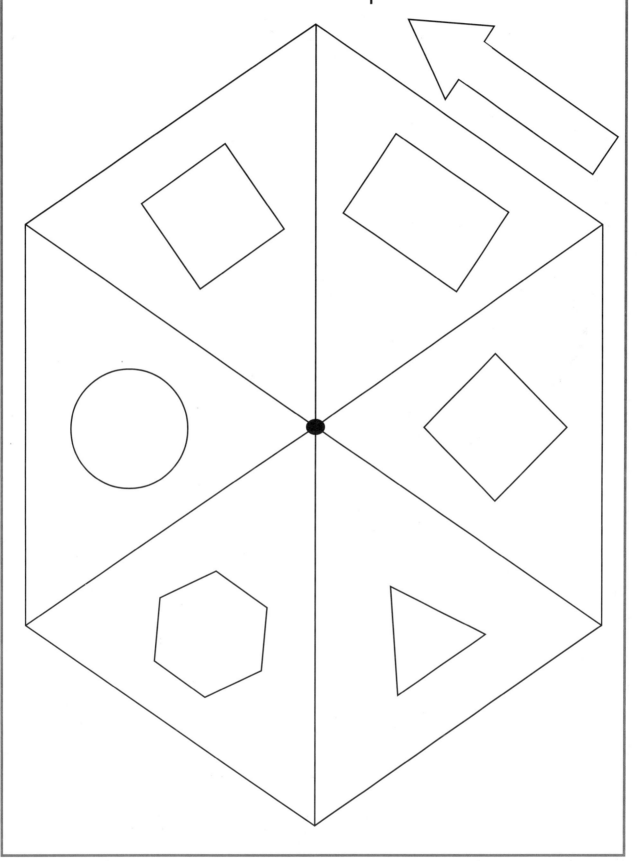

Butterfly patterns

Draw patterns onto the wings. Make them the same on each wing.

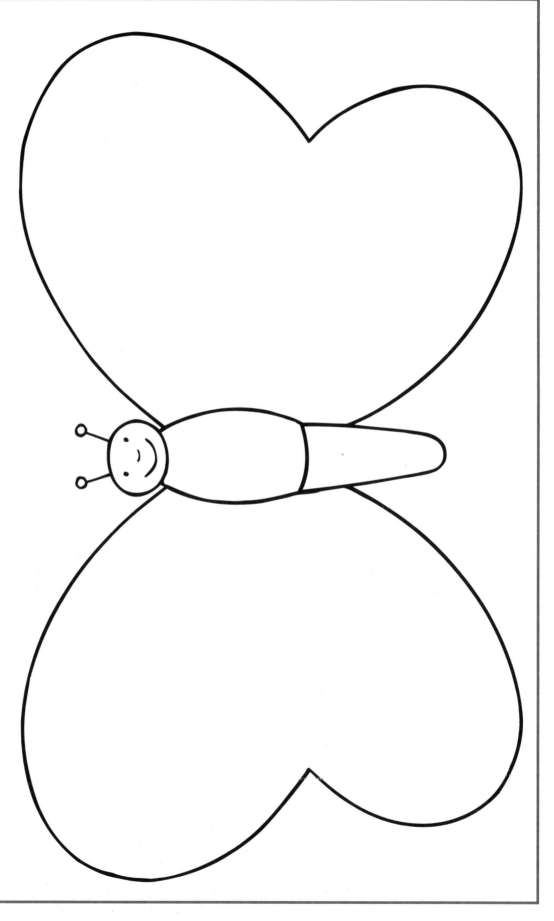

PEOPLE WHO HELP US

Learning objective
To listen attentively and talk about experiences in a group situation. (Language and Literacy)
Group size
Whole group.

PAGE 46
PEOPLE POSTER

Enlarge a copy of the photocopiable sheet and show it to the children as a way of introducing or consolidating the topic. Can the children recognize who the people are? How do these people help others? Use the opportunity to dispel stereotyped images. For example, ensure that the children understand that men as well as women can be nurses and so on. Ask individual children to choose a person from the sheet and without telling the others who it is, mime a helping action for the others to guess.

Learning objective
To develop vocabulary and increase confidence and fluency when speaking. (Language and Literacy)
Group size
Up to six children.

PAGE 47
EMERGENCY

Find out what the children know about emergency vehicles. Do they know the name of the vehicle that takes sick people to the hospital? What do firefighters travel in? Give each child a copy of the photocopiable sheet and ask individuals or pairs to tell you about their chosen picture. Encourage the others in the group to listen carefully. Now choose one of the vehicles and invite the children to make up a special rescue story. Help them to structure their story by asking questions such as, 'What happened next?' 'Where did it happen?' and so on. Scribe the children's story and ask them to illustrate it.

PAGE 48
MAKE IT BETTER

Ask the children to tell you about a time when they were sad. Did anyone help them and make them feel better? How? Give each child a copy of the photocopiable sheet. What is happening in the pictures? Why are the children in the pictures sad? Can the children think of a way to make each of the children in the pictures feel happy again? Ask older children to draw the next picture or pictures in the sequence.

Learning objective
To make up simple endings for stories, using pictures as a stimulus. (Language and Literacy)
Group size
Small groups.

PAGE 49
FRIENDS

Ask the children to tell you about one of their friends. Why do they like their friend? What things do they like doing together? Why is it important to help each other? Give each child a copy of the photocopiable sheet and ask them to look carefully at the pictures. Decide, as a group, what order the pictures should go in. Ask the children to cut out the pictures and arrange them in the correct order. Ask each child in turn to describe the next picture in the sequence. When the story is finished, ask the children to talk about times when they have helped or been helped by a friend. Invite older children to draw at least two pictures of their own to show how they helped (or were helped by) their friend.

Learning objective
To develop sequencing skills. (Language and Literacy)
Group size
Four children.

PAGE 50
PEOPLE PUZZLES

Learning objective
To develop matching and shape recognition skills. (Mathematical Development)
Group size
Individuals.

Copy the photocopiable sheet onto card for each child and explain that the sheet provides four two-piece puzzles. Tell the children that you would like them to look at the pictures and match the correct object to the person. Encourage the children to talk about each of the pictures as they match the pieces. Suggest that older children make some more two-piece puzzles by drawing on the reverse side of the pieces. Encourage the children to swap puzzles with their friends.

PAGE 51
WASHING DAY

Learning objective
To develop number recognition and counting skills. (Mathematical Development)
Group size
Small groups.

Ask the children to tell you about the jobs that people do at home. What jobs do they like to help with at home? Give each child a copy of the photocopiable sheet and explain that the washing has been muddled up and needs to be hung on the washing line in number order. Ask the children to cut-out the washing, read out the numbers on each item and try to arrange them in the correct sequence on a piece of paper. Blank out the numbers for younger children and concentrate on developing one-to-one correspondence and counting skills. Ask older children to add extra items to take the washing number line up to ten.

PAGE 52
SORT THE POST

Learning objective
To develop sorting skills using everyday objects. (Mathematical Development)
Group size
Small groups.

Fill a large sack with letters, postcards and parcels in a variety of different shapes and sizes. Let the children empty the sack and ask them to practise sorting the post in different ways. Ask them to explain why they have sorted the post in that particular way. Provide each child with a copy of the photocopiable sheet and ask them to cut out the pictures and then stick them in sets onto a blank piece of paper. Can the children describe the way in which they have sorted the different items?

PAGE 53
CERTIFICATE

Learning objective
To celebrate achievement. (Personal, Social and Emotional Development)
Group size
Individuals.

Use the photocopiable sheet as a special reward certificate for children who have shown particular care for others. Copy it onto card or coloured paper and present it to the individuals at a group or circle time. Encourage the other children to say 'Well done!' or to clap. This will give the children a sense of self esteem and pride in their achievements. Let the children take home their certificates to show to their parents and carers.

PAGE 54
I CAN HELP

Learning objective
To treat property and the environment with care and concern. (Personal, Social and Emotional Development)
Group size
Whole group.

Make sure that the children are involved in your tidy-up sessions. Encourage them to store toys and equipment in labelled boxes and trays, and to establish monitors who take it in turns to do specific jobs, such as sweeping up the sand or pegging up the aprons. At circle time, display an enlarged copy of the photocopiable sheet on an easel or board and ask the children to describe the messy things in the pictures. What would they do to clean them up? Ask individual children to come to the front and draw arrows between the messy things and the ways to make them tidy again.

PAGE 55
NO MORE RUBBISH

Learning objective
To talk about the local environment. (Knowledge and Understanding of the World)
Group size
Up to six children.

Enlarge a copy of the photocopiable sheet and ask the children to look at it carefully with you. Can anyone tell you why the park keeper is looking unhappy? (Because of the litter that people have dropped.) Why should we always put litter into bins? What would our parks and towns look like if we all just dropped our litter on the ground instead of putting it in a bin? Give each child a copy of the photocopiable sheet and ask them to find the litter on the picture and circle it to help the park keeper to keep the park clean. Invite older children to make a poster telling people not to drop litter.

PAGE 56

ANIMALS THAT HELP US

Learning objective
To learn about ways that animals help us. (Knowledge and Understanding of the World)
Group size
Whole group.

If possible, arrange for a police officer and a police dog, or someone from the Guide Dogs for the Blind Association to come in to your setting and talk to the children about their work, and the way that the animals are trained. Encourage the children to ask questions about the jobs that the animals do. Show the children a copy of the photocopiable sheet and talk about the pictures together. Explain the type of work that each animal does. Ask older children to make up a story that includes one of the animals. Scribe it for them if necessary and share the stories at circle time.

PAGE 57

A HELPING HAND

Learning objective
To move with confidence and imagination. (Physical Development)
Group size
Up to four children.

Enlarge a copy of the photocopiable sheet onto card. Provide a counter for each child and a dice numbered 1–3. Let the children take it in turns to throw the dice and move around the board. When they land on a picture, they must identify it and mime an action or series of movements to show what the person does. The winner is the first child to reach home, but before they can win, they must mime an action of something that they do to help at home for the others to guess. Let younger children copy your mimes if they need help.

PAGE 58

PEOPLE PUPPETS

Learning objective
To make puppets to use in imaginative play. (Creative Development)
Group size
Individuals; small groups.

Copy the photocopiable sheet and make the two puppets. Talk to the children about road safety and remind them of how a police officer and a crossing patrol person are there to help them to keep safe. Enact some road-crossing scenarios for the children, using the puppets, or use them as you sing some road safety songs – a selection can be found in *This Little Puffin* compiled by Elizabeth Matterson (Puffin). Provide each child with a copy of the photocopiable sheet and show them how to fold, stick and colour the puppets. Encourage them to use the puppets in their imaginative play, such as with small-world toys and road playmats.

PAGE 59

DRESSING-UP

Learning objective
To develop imaginative play. (Creative Development)
Group size
Pairs.

Set up your role-play area as a hospital. Provide a selection of doctors' and nurses' clothes and equipment and encourage the children's play by going into role with them. Suggest a range of different scenarios for the children to act out and show them how to fill out medical records and care for their patients! Copy the photocopiable sheet onto card and let each pair of children cut, stick and make the wrist and headbands for use in their play. Fill out the details on the wristband for younger children.

PAGE 60

AT THE CLINIC

Learning objective
To develop ability to use imagination. (Creative Development)
Group size
Up to four children.

Set up the role-play area as a baby clinic. Provide weighing scales, baby baths, tape-measures and other safe baby equipment (such as empty plastic talcum powder bottles). Encourage the children to take it in turns to use the area, bringing in a baby doll to be weighed and measured. Show the children how to use the equipment and provide them with copies of the photocopiable sheet to fill in. Demonstrate to the children how to draw the baby's picture and fill in the details. Let younger children take part in some play writing. Encourage older children to weigh and measure the 'babies' accurately.

People poster

◆ Talk about these people who help us.

Emergency

◆ Who uses these vehicles? How do they help us?

Make it better

◆ Why do these children need help?
How would you help them?

Friends

◆ Cut out the pictures and put them in the correct order to tell the story.

People puzzles

◆ Cut out and match the puzzle pieces.

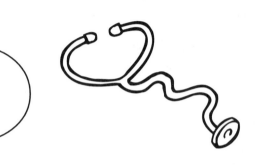

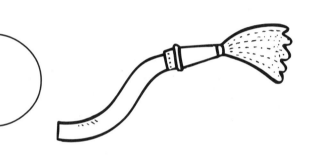

ADCEPXL
BMJHCIGT
FDENOLKMJS
TOBWXZECDAM
RKLOHDPQMSUFW

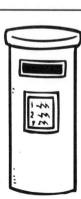

Washing day

◆ Cut out the washing. Hang it on the line in number order.

Sort the post

◆ Cut out the post and sort it into sets.

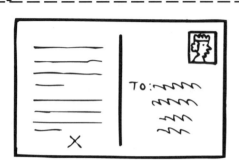

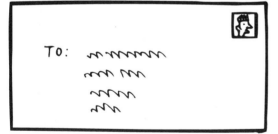
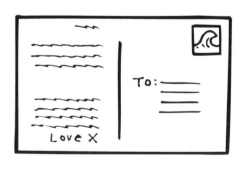

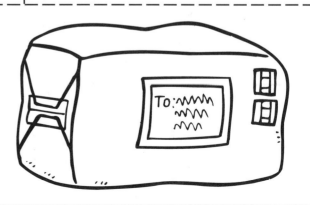

Certificate

Certificate

This certificate has been awarded to:

For being very helpful by:

on:

signed:

I can help

◆ Help to tidy up by drawing arrows to match the objects.

No more rubbish

◆ Find the rubbish and circle it to help the park keeper.

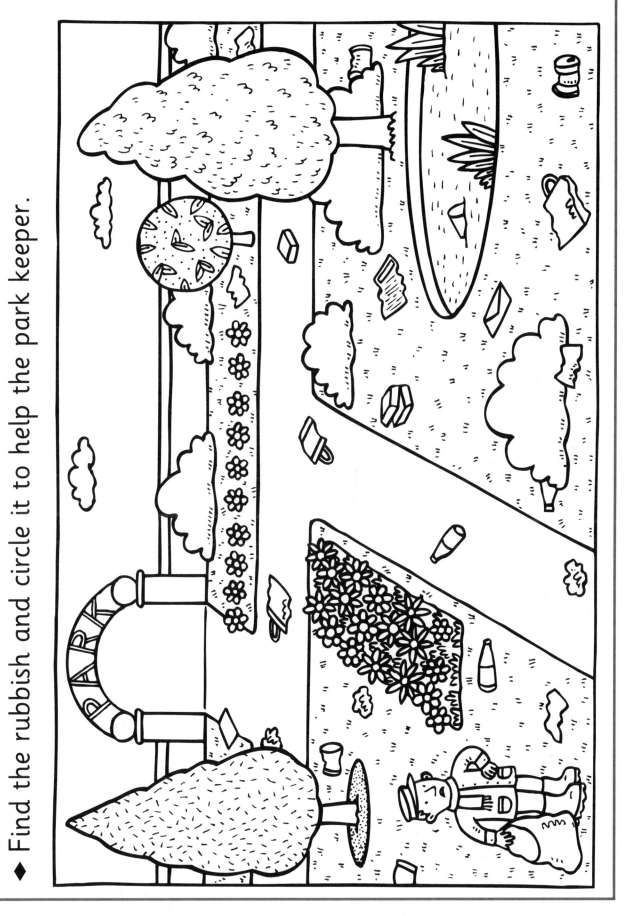

Animals that help us

◆ Talk about the pictures and how these animals help us.

A helping hand

◆ Throw the dice and move around the board. Mime the actions of the person you have landed on.

People puppets

◆ Cut out and stick together to make finger puppets. Use them to play games.

Dressing-up

◆ Use these things to play doctors and nurses.

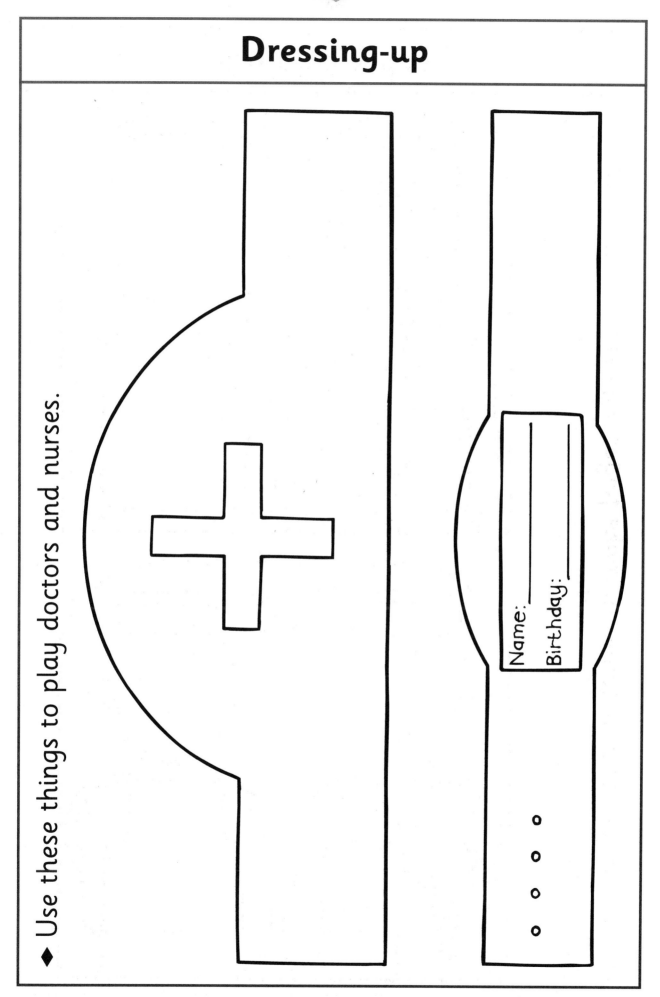

Name: _____

Birthday: _____

At the clinic

◆ Use this card for your baby clinic.

Baby record

name: _____

age: _____

weight: _____

height: _____

notes: _____

_____

JOURNEYS

PAGE 64
LIFT-THE-FLAP

Learning objective
To use pictures and symbols to communicate meaning. (Language and Literacy)
Group size
Up to six children.

Ask the children to tell you about any long journeys that they have made. How did they get there? What is their favourite way to travel? Give each child a copy of the photocopiable sheet and ask them to cut out the pictures and use sticky tape to fix one edge of each picture to a separate sheet of paper. Together, talk about where the plane or bus might be going. Encourage the children to use their imaginations and to draw pictures of their chosen imaginary places under the flaps.

PAGE 65
FOLLOW THE TRAIL

Learning objective
To develop pre-writing skills. (Language and Literacy)
Group size
Whole group; individuals.

Find a large open space and explain to the children that you would like them to think about the different ways that they can move around on their feet. Ask them to skip, shuffle, stamp, tiptoe and so on. After each movement, make some marks on a piece of paper to represent the different walks, such as up and down marks for skipping or zigzag marks for stamping. Give each child a copy of the photocopiable sheet and ask them to trace the lines with their fingers. Do they think the person is stamping, skipping or running? Now ask them to draw in between each of the lines to follow the different trails.

PAGE 66
AT THE PARK

Learning objective
To develop letter sound recognition. (Language and Literacy)
Group size
Small groups.

If possible, use the photocopiable sheet after a group outing to the park. Spend some time talking about the picture. Ask individual children to point to an object in the picture and tell you what it is. Can the children hear the letter sound at the start of the word? Find an object beginning with 'p' and say it aloud for the children. Help them to repeat the word, emphasizing the letter sound. Can anyone find another word that begins with that sound? As a group, let the children try to find all the 'p' words and circle or colour them in. Invite older children to find the objects unaided.

PAGE 67
PACK THE BAG

Learning objective
To develop letter sound recognition. (Language and Literacy)
Group size
Small groups.

Gather together a selection of holiday objects such as sun-glasses, sun cream and sandwiches and put them in a suitcase. Describe them one at a time to the children, for example, 'I begin with an 's'. People wear me to stop the sun hurting their eyes. What am I?'. Provide each child with a copy of the photocopiable sheet and ask them to cut out the objects beginning with 'b' and stick them into the bag. Help younger children by saying the names of the objects together, emphasizing the initial sounds.

PAGE 68
COUNT THE PASSENGERS

Learning objective
To develop awareness of number operations and to use appropriate vocabulary. (Mathematical Development)
Group size
Small groups.

The photocopiable sheet may be used to reinforce a number of different maths concepts. For example:
• Counting – ask younger children to draw a given number of passengers on each train.
• Number bonds – choose a number such as five, and ask older children to draw five passengers on each of the three trains. Ask them to put some passengers in the first carriage and the rest in the second carriage. Can they share the five passengers differently in each train? Provide extra copies of the photocopiable sheet to record other ways of sharing.
• Odds and evens – investigate different numbers. 'Which numbers can be shared equally between the two carriages?'

PAGE 69

AIR, LAND OR SEA?

Learning objective
To develop sorting skills. (Mathematical Development)
Group size
Small groups.

Provide each child with a copy of the photocopiable sheet and together talk about the different types of transport. Which things travel in the sea? In the air? On land? Ask the children to cut out the pictures and sort them into three sets. Encourage older children to draw some more pictures to go with each of the sets. Now invite the children to choose one of the sets and to draw an appropriate background picture to stick them on to.

PAGE 70

JOURNEY TO THE MOON

Learning objective
To develop counting skills. (Mathematical Development)
Group size
Pairs.

Copy the photocopiable sheet onto a sheet of thin card and invite the children to colour it in. Laminate it if possible. Provide a counter for each child and a 1–3 dot dice. Explain that the object of the game is to reach the moon by moving the counters after each throw of the dice. If older children land on a star they must try to work out what number is hidden underneath the star before they can take their next turn. Help younger children to develop counting skills by encouraging them to count the dots on the dice and by guiding them as they move their counters up the board.

PAGE 71

A WORLD OF FOOD

Learning objective
To develop knowledge of other cultures. (Personal, Social and Emotional Development)
Group size
Whole group.

Enlarge a copy of the photocopiable sheet and show it to the children. Do they recognize any of the foods. What do they know about them? What foods do they like to eat? Explain that these foods have been transported from other countries and have made long journeys in boats, lorries or aeroplanes. Arrange to have a 'World Food Day' by inviting parents and carers to cook dishes from their own or other cultures and by cooking some multicultural foods with your group. Display all the foods and encourage the children to taste them. (NB Be aware of any food allergies and ask parents to clearly label the ingredients used.)

PAGE 72

LOCAL JOURNEY

Learning objective
To talk and learn about the local area. (Knowledge and Understanding of the World)
Group size
Whole group, plus adult helpers.

Take the children out for a walk in the local area. Provide each child with a copy of the photocopiable sheet, a clipboard and pencil, and ask them to look carefully for the objects on their sheet. When the children have found each one, ask them to tick the list and to draw a picture to show the object in its setting. Is it a busy road with parked cars? Is the post-box near some houses? Encourage older children to find two more objects to draw on the reverse of the photocopiable sheet. Back inside, talk about the things that the children noticed and use the opportunity to increase their geographical vocabulary.

PAGE 73

ON THE MAP

Learning objective
To explore and recognize features of living things and objects in the natural and made world. (Knowledge and Understanding of the World)
Group size
Small groups.

Provide each child with a copy of the photocopiable sheet and ask them to talk about the different signs, symbols and features that they can see. Encourage the children to use the correct geographical vocabulary. Explain that you would like them to cut out the pictures and stick them in the appropriate places. Where could the zebra crossing be placed? Which road do they think is the High Street? Encourage older children to add some extra features to the map such as shops, signs, pedestrians and vehicles.

PAGE 74

PICTURE POSTCARDS

Learning objective
To talk about past events in their own lives. (Knowledge and Understanding of the World)
Group size
Small groups.

Enlarge the photocopiable sheet to A3 size and either stick or copy it onto card. The postcards show scenes which will be familiar to many of the children. Encourage the children to relate the pictures to their own experiences. Cut out the postcards and invite children to choose one of the pictures to colour in. Invite older children to write about their real or imaginary experience on the back of the postcard and scribe the words for younger children. Provide a supply of the postcards for the children to use in the writing area.

PAGE 75
TRANSPORT

Learning objective
To use construction materials with increasing skill and control. (Physical Development)
Group size
Individuals; small groups.

If possible, enlarge a copy of the photocopiable sheet and talk about the different models with the children. Do they recognize any of the materials used (such as Lego, Mobilo and Sticklebricks)? Explain that the models are all types of transport. How many different types of vehicle can they see? Let the children select a model and the appropriate construction materials and ask them to try to copy the shapes. Invite older children to make up their own transport model and suggest that they draw it on a separate sheet of paper for others to copy.

PAGE 76
FLYING HIGH

Learning objective
To use tools and objects safely and with increasing control. (Physical Development)
Group size
Up to four children.

Copy the photocopiable sheet onto card for each child. Invite the children to cut out the three sections and to colour them imaginatively. If possible, show them some pictures of real aeroplanes, drawing their attention to the designs and motifs. Help them to make small slits where indicated and show them how to 'thread' the wing pieces through. Arrange to take the aeroplanes to a safe open space for the children to try them out. To make the planes into mobiles, punch holes in the nose and tail of the planes, thread wool through each hole and attach the wool to a washing line strung across your room.

PAGE 77
STORYBOARD

Tell the children a version of the tale 'The Three Billy Goats Gruff' (Traditional). Enlarge a copy of the photocopiable sheet and stick it onto a piece of stiff card. Invite a small group of children to help you to decorate it with colours and collage materials. Laminate the finished picture. Remind the children of the story and explain that this storyboard can be used with puppets (see below) to retell the story. Provide individual children with their own copy of the sheet to decorate. They may wish to draw the characters onto the sheet or to use it with their own set of puppets (see below).

Learning objective
To develop imagination and to respond to a well-known story. (Creative Development)
Group size
Whole group; small groups; individuals.

PAGE 78
BILLY GOAT PUPPETS

Remind the children of the story of 'The Three Billy Goats Gruff' (Traditional). Explain that you are going to help them to make finger puppets of the goats and the troll. Help younger children to cut out the figures and encourage all the children to decorate or colour them in. Show them how to fit the tabs around their fingers using sticky tape, providing help where necessary. If the children have made their own storyboards, or if you have a group storyboard (see above), encourage them to use their puppets in conjunction with it to tell the story.

Learning objective
To develop imagination and to respond to a well-known story. (Creative Development)
Group size
Small groups.

Lift-the-flap

◆ Cut out and make lift-the-flap pictures.

Follow the trail

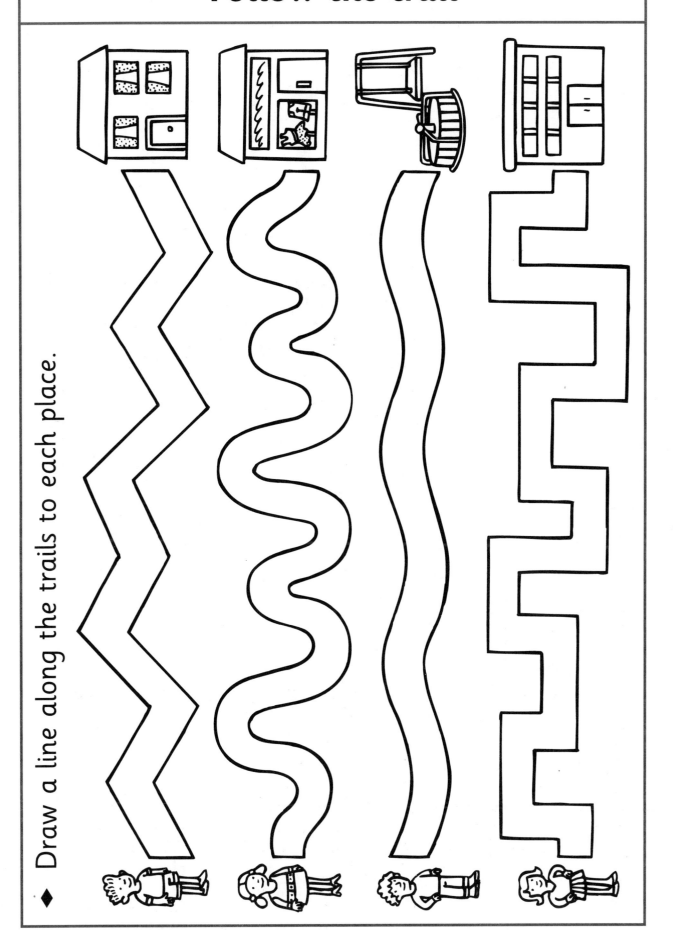

◆ Draw a line along the trails to each place.

At the park

◆ Find the things beginning with 'p'.

Pack the bag

◆ Cut out the pictures. Put the things beginning with 'b' in the bag.

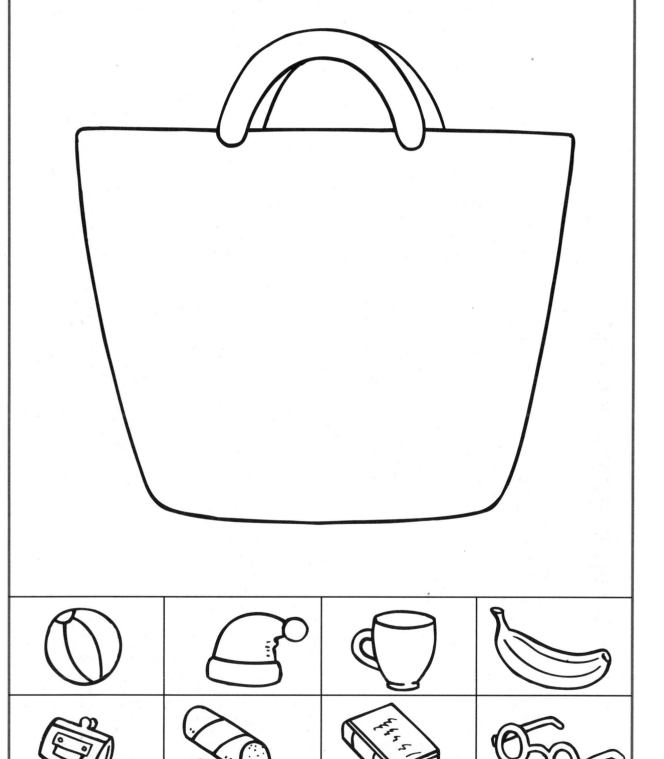

Count the passengers

◆ Put _____ passengers on the train.

Air, land or sea?

◆ Cut out the pictures. Sort them into sets.

Journey to the moon

◆ Throw a dice and move your counter to the moon!

A world of food

◆ Talk about these foods. Where do they come from?

Local journey

◆ Can you find these things in your local area?
Draw pictures to show where you found them.

object	tick	drawing
road		
post-box		
lamppost		

On the map

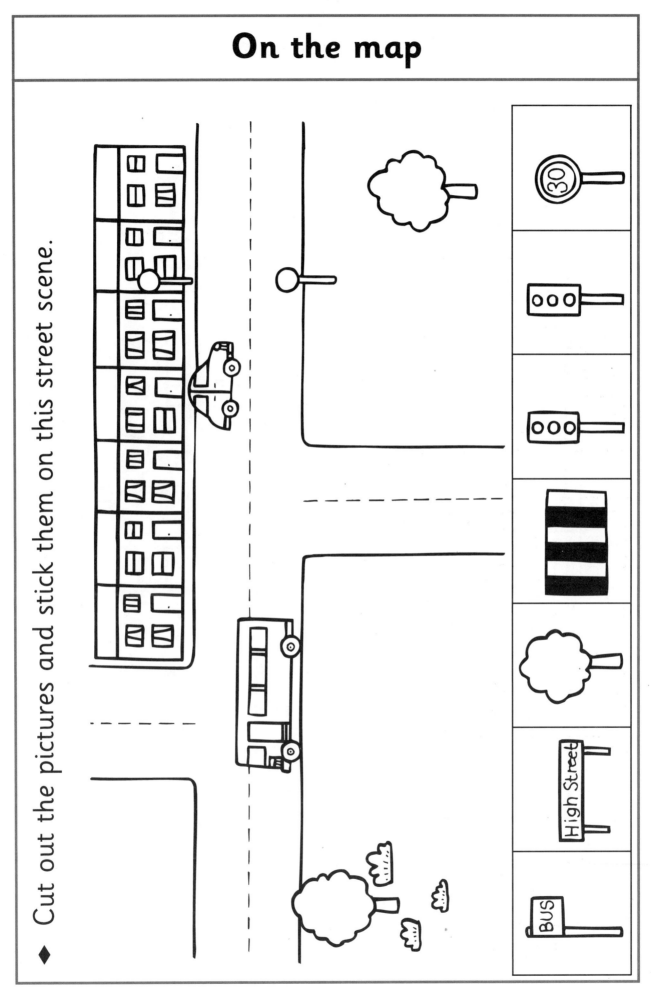

◆ Cut out the pictures and stick them on this street scene.

Picture postcards

♦ Talk about the pictures. Cut out and send one to a friend.

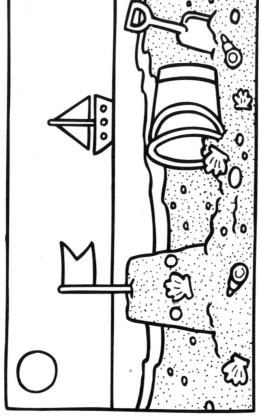

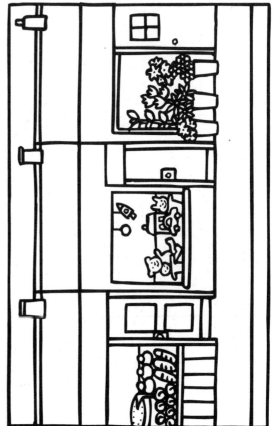

Transipport

◆ Try to make one of these models. Now make one of your own and draw it.

Flying high

Cut out the pieces and join together to make an aeroplane.

Storyboard

◆ Decorate the picture. Use it to tell the story of The Three Billy Goats Gruff.

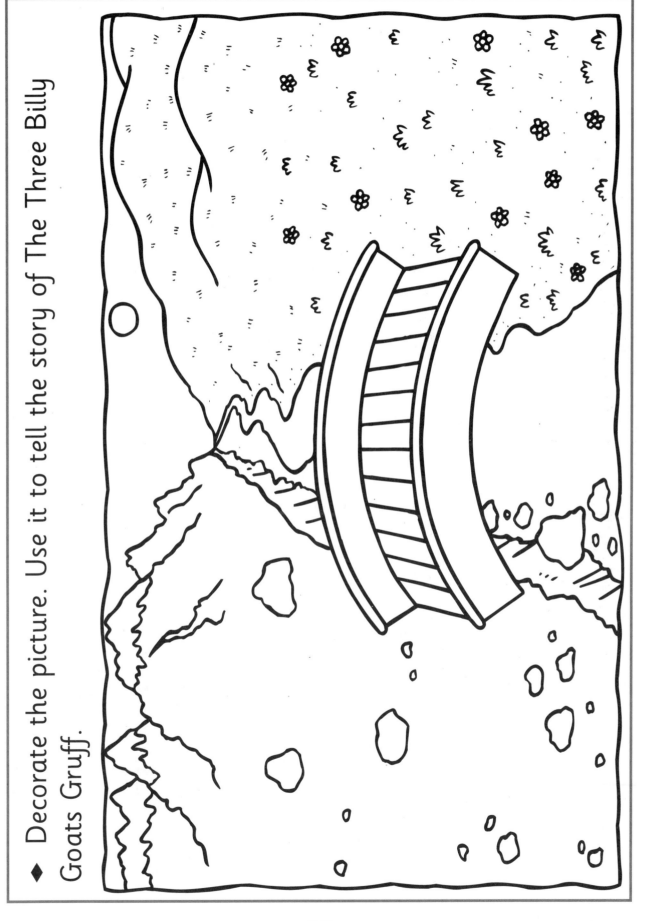

Billy goat puppets

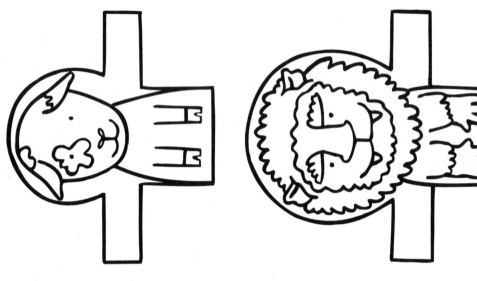

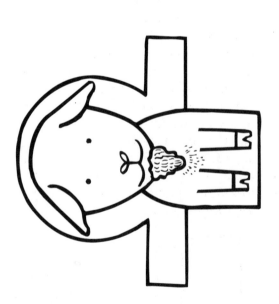

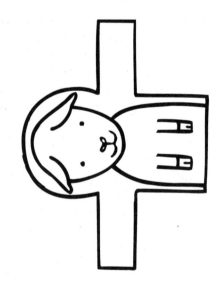

◆ Cut out, colour and make finger puppets.

WEATHER

PAGE 82
INCY WINCY SPIDER

Learning objective
To respond to a familiar rhyme and develop sequencing skills. (Language and Literacy)
Group size
Small groups.

Tell the children the rhyme, 'Incy Wincy Spider climbed up the water spout' in *This Little Puffin*, compiled by Elizabeth Matterson (Puffin). Give each child a copy of the photocopiable sheet which has six pictures that tell the rhyme. Ask the children to cut out the pictures in three horizontal strips (two pictures per strip) and show them how to glue the three strips together, back to back, to make a circular book (see diagram on the photocopiable sheet). Now ask the children to decorate the pictures and tell the rhyme, using the pictures to help them. Do they notice how the rhyme continues? The beginning and ending of the rhyme are almost the same.

PAGE 83
WET AND DRY

Learning objective
To use symbols and pictures to communicate meaning. (Language and Literacy)
Group size
Small groups.

Ask the children to tell you about the clothes that they wear in different types of weather. Show them some clothes, such as a sun-hat and raincoat. Can the children tell you when they would wear them? Give each child a copy of the photocopiable sheet and ask them to cut out the two pictures. When would the children use these things? Show the children how to stick one edge of each of the pictures to a separate sheet of paper. Encourage them to draw a picture of themselves in sunny or rainy day clothes under the appropriate flaps.

PAGE 84
WEATHER DICE

Give each child a copy of the photocopiable sheet. 'Read' the symbols together then encourage them to colour the symbols. Help the children to assemble their dice. Use the dice to play a dressing-up game. Sit in a circle and place sun-glasses and sun-hat (sun); wellies and umbrella (rain); scarf, hat and gloves (snow) in the centre. Let the children take it in turns to throw their dice, 'read' the symbol and put on the matching clothes. Encourage older children to explain their choice and to say something about the weather such as, 'I wear wellies in the rain to keep my feet dry. I like splashing in the puddles'. Ask younger children questions to help them find the matching clothes such as, 'What might keep your hands warm when it is cold and snowy?'.

PAGE 85
NURSERY RHYME SPINNER

Enlarge or stick the photocopiable sheet onto card. Let individual children colour the pictures. Pierce a hole in the centre of the spinner. Cut out the arrow shape and attach it to the centre of the spinner with a split pin. The rhymes on the spinner are all linked to the weather – 'Incy Wincy Spider'; 'Doctor Foster'; 'I Hear Thunder' and 'Here We Go Round the Mulberry Bush'. Use the spinner as a regular feature of your circle time, letting a different child spin it each time. Ask the child to 'read' the picture and tell the group which rhyme to sing next.

Learning objective
To develop pre-reading, observation and matching skills. (Language and Literacy)
Group size
Small groups.

Learning objective
To develop knowledge of rhyme and pattern in language and to develop pre-reading skills. (Language and Literacy)
Group size
Whole group.

PAGE 86

SCARF PATTERNS

Introduce the idea of patterns on the children's clothes. What patterns can they see? Ask the children to contribute ideas and draw their attention to simple repeating patterns. Provide a tray of interlocking cubes such as Unifix or Multilink and encourage the children to watch as you start a two-colour pattern. Can they tell you what colour to put next? Let the children take turns to start a pattern for others to guess. Give each child a copy of the photocopiable sheet and explain that you would like them to colour repeating patterns onto the scarves. Ask older children to use at least three colours.

PAGE 87

UMBRELLAS

Provide each child with a copy of the photocopiable sheet and explain that you would like them to design as many different umbrellas as possible using just three colours. Show them how each umbrella has three sections and explain that they may only use one colour per section. Suggest that they make each umbrella look different by changing the order of the colours, such as 'red, yellow and blue' and 'yellow, blue and red'. They may also use each colour more than once. Provide older children with extra copies of the sheet and encourage them to find as many combinations as they can.

PAGE 88

WEATHER WEAR

Tell the children the traditional story of 'Goldilocks and the Three Bears'. Ask them to help you to remember the different sizes of the bears and their belongings. Give each child a copy of the photocopiable sheet. Explain that it is cold outside and that two of the bears have got their clothes muddled up and need help to find the right things. Ask the children to draw arrows between the bears and their matching clothes. Invite older children to draw a different-sized bear and a set of matching clothes.

PAGE 89

SNOWMEN

Provide a dice with dots from 1–6 for the group and a copy of the photocopiable sheet for each child. Explain that the snowmen are each wearing a different number of buttons and that the object of the game is to take it in turns to throw the dice, count the dots and cover up the snowman that matches. Provide younger children with a 1–3 dot dice and white-out the extra buttons. Encourage them to point to each dot as they count, to help them to develop one-to-one correspondence.

PAGE 90

DRESSING BEAR

Enlarge a copy of the photocopiable sheet and introduce the bear to the group. Explain that he is a weather bear and needs to be dressed in clothes suitable for the day's weather. What is the weather like today? Can the children think of something for him to wear? Choose a child to dress the bear using colours or collage materials. Let the child take the bear home with him or her. Use this as a regular feature of your day, choosing a different child to dress the bear each time.

PAGE 91

WEATHER CHART

The photocopiable sheet can be used flexibly as part of your routine for observing and recording the weather. It may be enlarged, photocopied onto card, coloured and laminated for use with the whole group or may be used in its A4 format as a weekly record that is kept and filed in a weather book. Alternatively, you could give individual children their own recording sheet. Fill the blank squares with pictures chosen from the activity sheet 'Weather symbols' (on page 92), illustrations drawn by the children or words – either scribed by you or an older child's emergent writing.

PAGE 92
WEATHER SYMBOLS

The photocopiable sheet is designed to be used in conjunction with the 'Weather chart' on page 91. Copy it onto card and, if you have enlarged the chart, enlarge the symbols to fit in the blank spaces. Ask the children to colour the pictures. Invite individual children to choose the most appropriate card for the day's weather and to attach the card to the chart using Velcro or Blu-Tack. For individual recording, let the children colour their pictures and glue them onto their chart. Suggest that older children make an envelope to store their unused pictures for another time.

PAGE 93
WINDMILL

Provide each child with a copy of the photocopiable sheet and help them to cut out and fold the windmill as indicated. Fix the ends of the folded sections with a small piece of sticky tape and help the children to use a split pin to attach the windmill to a plastic Artstraw. Show the children how to blow the windmill to make it move and take them outside to watch the windmills move in the breeze. Extend the activity by encouraging the children to spin and move like a windmill, speeding up and slowing down as the wind changes pace.

PAGE 94
SOUNDS LIKE RAIN

Ask the children to think about the noises that different types of weather make, such as thunder crashing and wind howling. Provide a selection of percussion instruments and listen to them one by one. Do any of the sounds remind them of the weather? Say the name of a type of weather such as thunder, and invite a child to choose an instrument to represent the sound. Now show the children the photocopiable sheet and 'read' the weather pictures. Give each child an instrument and explain that when you

hold up their matching weather symbol you would like them to play their instrument. Let older children use the symbols to make up a sequence of weather sounds to copy.

PAGE 95
SUN-HAT

Provide each child with a copy of the photocopiable sheet, enlarged to A3 size and copied or stuck onto card. Help the children to cut out the shape and ask them to decorate their sunflower with coloured pens or pencils and collage materials. Help them to fit the hat by stapling elastic or ribbon to the sides to tie under the chin. Use the opportunity to remind the children about covering up in the sun.

PAGE 96
SEASIDE KIOSK

Set up the role-play area as a seaside café. Make a kiosk removing the bottom from a large cardboard box, turning it on its side and covering it with brightly-coloured paint or paper. Provide a table and chairs, crockery, menus and waiter/waitress aprons. Provide copies of the photocopiable sheet for the children to use. Talk about the prices with the children and encourage them to add to the menu. Let the children use Plasticine or pretend fruit and food and encourage them to take turns to serve each other dishes from the menu!

Incy Wincy Spider

◆ Cut out and stick together to make a nursery rhyme book.

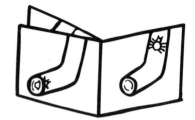

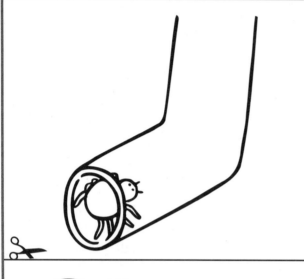

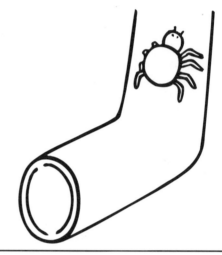

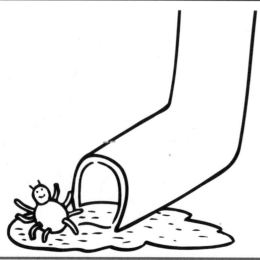

Wet and dry

◆ Cut out, colour and make lift-the-flap pictures.

Weather dice

◆ Colour and cut out to make your own weather dice.

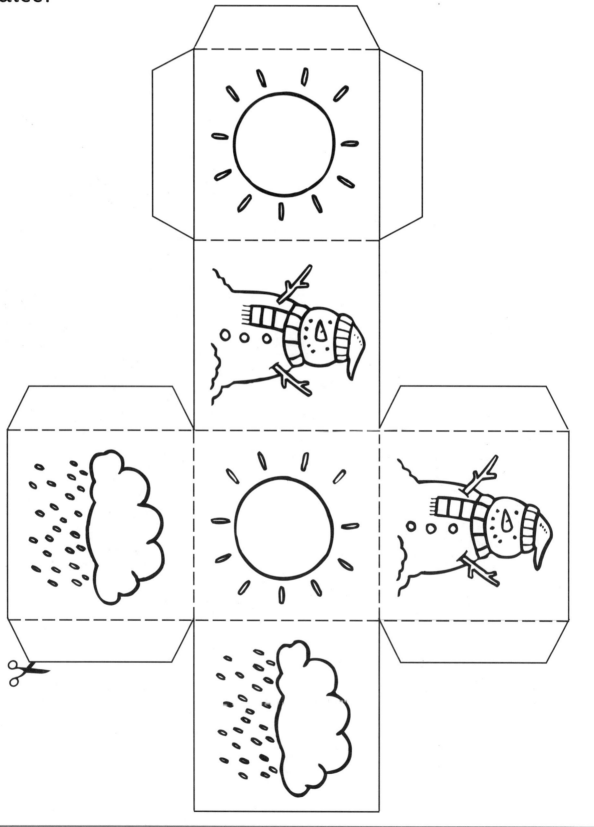

Nursery rhyme spinner

◆ Cut out to make a spinner.

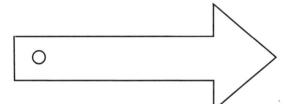

Scarf patterns

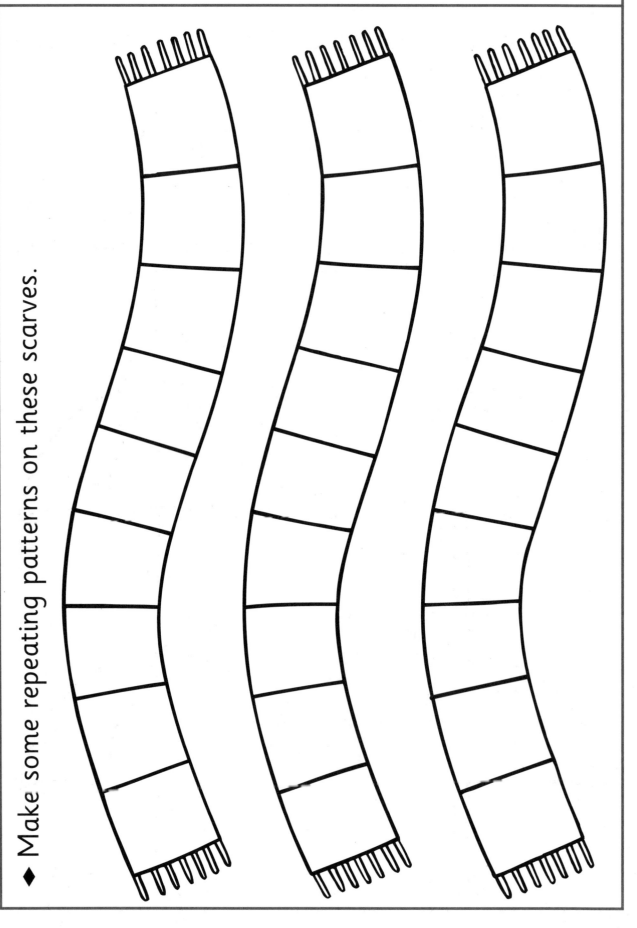

◆ Make some repeating patterns on these scarves.

Umbrellas

◆ Use three colours and make each umbrella look different.

Weather wear

◆ Draw arrows to match clothes to the bears.

Snowmen

◆ Count the buttons on the snowmen.

Dressing bear

◆ Draw some clothes for the bear.

Weather chart

Our weather chart				
Monday	Today it is			
Tuesday	Today it is			
Wednesday	Today it is			
Thursday	Today it is			
Friday	Today it is			

Weather symbols

◆ Cut out the pictures and use them to record the weather.

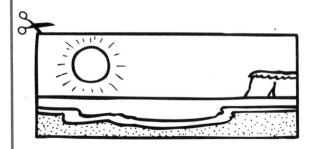

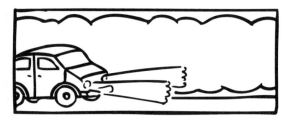

Windmill

◆ Cut out, decorate and fold to make a windmill. Attach it to a stick.

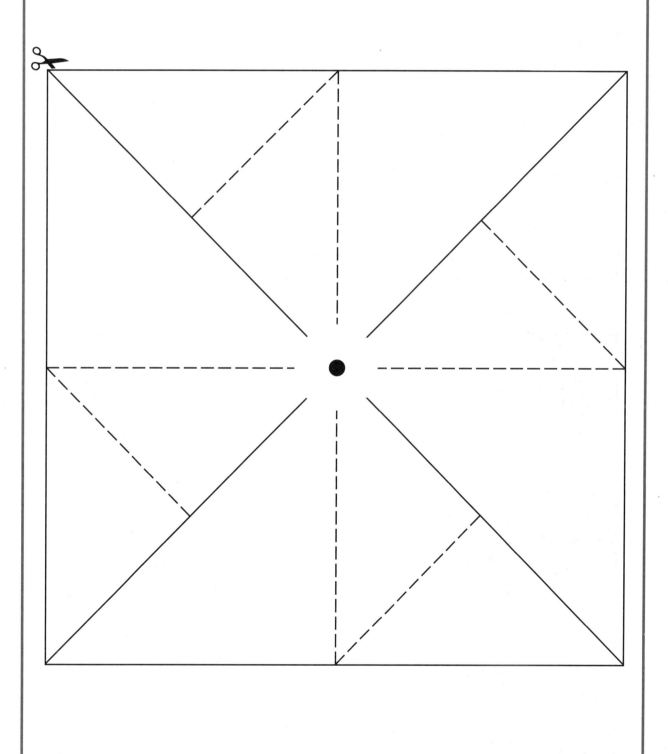

Sounds like rain

◆ Use the weather symbols to make up some weather music.

Sun-hat

◆ Cut out, decorate and make into a sun-hat.

Seaside kiosk

Ice-cream menu

1 scoop		30p
2 scoops		40p
banana split		80p
ice-cream special		80p
lollipop		30p
ice-cream sandwich		50p